YO-YO MAKER

Pedro Flores

PAIGE V. POLINSKY

Checkerboard
Library

An Imprint of Abdo Publishing
abdopublishing.com

abdopublishing.com

Published by Abdo Publishing, a division of ABDO, PO Box 398166, Minneapolis, Minnesota 55439. Copyright © 2018 by Abdo Consulting Group, Inc. International copyrights reserved in all countries. No part of this book may be reproduced in any form without written permission from the publisher. Checkerboard Library™ is a trademark and logo of Abdo Publishing.

Printed in the United States of America, North Mankato, Minnesota
062017
092017

THIS BOOK CONTAINS
RECYCLED MATERIALS

Design and Production: Mighty Media, Inc.
Editor: Rebecca Felix
Cover Photographs: Courtesy Jo Ann Radovan (center); Mighty Media, Inc. (border)
Interior Photographs: Alamy, p. 19; AP Images, pp. 21, 27; David Hall/Museum of Yo-Yo History, p. 12; Getty Images, p. 15; iStockphoto, p. 5; Lars Hundley, pp. 13, 28 (right); Mighty Media, Inc., p. 11; Rick Brough, pp. 9, 14; Shutterstock, pp. 4, 7, 8, 23, 29 (top & bottom right); Steve Vesper, pp. 17, 29 (bottom left); Wikimedia Commons, pp. 10, 28 (left); Wisconsin Historical Society, WHS-1978.404.42 & WHS-2001.83.13, p. 25; Yoyos 4 Africa, p. 26

Publisher's Cataloging-in-Publication Data
Names: Polinsky, Paige V., author.
Title: Yo-yo maker: Pedro Flores / by Paige V. Polinsky.
Other titles: Pedro Flores
Description: Minneapolis, MN : Abdo Publishing, 2018. | Series: Toy trailblazers | Includes bibliographical references and index.
Identifiers: LCCN 2016962803 | ISBN 9781532110993 (lib. bdg.) | ISBN 9781680788846 (ebook)
Subjects: LCSH: Flores, Pedro--Juvenile literature. | Yo-yo (Toy)--Juvenile literature. | Toymakers--United States--Biography--Juvenile literature.
Classification: DDC 688.7/092 [B]--dc23
LC record available at http://lccn.loc.gov/2016962803

CONTENTS

Chapter 1

NEW LIFE

Pedro Flores was a passionate inventor and salesman. He brought new life to a toy that had been around since ancient times. He started the modern yo-yo **craze**! Pedro Edralin Flores was born on April 26, 1899, in the Philippines. He grew up in Vintar, a town in the Ilocos Norte **province**. Little is known about Pedro's family or early life.

The early 1900s were a difficult time in Pedro's homeland. The United States had just won the **Spanish-American War**. Before the war, Spain had ruled the Philippines. As part of the treaty, it gave the Philippines to the United States. But many Filipinos were tired of being ruled by another country. So, in 1899, a war began between the Philippines and the United States.

The **Philippine-American War** lasted three years. The United States won in 1902 and kept control of the Philippines. This brought changes to Pedro's hometown. It was **annexed** by the city of Bacarra for

Pedro Flores's hometown of Vintar is located on the Philippines' Luzon Island.

several years, only to break ties in 1908. Young Pedro's life continued to change. In 1915, he moved to the United States at the age of 16.

A BUSY *Student*

Flores was one of many US **immigrants** from the Philippines. Because their nation was under US control, Filipinos could travel to the United States easily. The United States also ran a Filipino education program. The program sent Filipino students to US schools. Some historians believe Flores may have been part of this program.

By 1919, Flores was living in California. He continued his education there into the 1920s. He attended San Francisco's High School of Commerce. Then, he enrolled in the University of California's law school. He later studied law at San Francisco State University.

Flores spent several years studying law. But he did not become a lawyer. Instead, he began working at a California hotel. Flores helped

**FUN FACT**

California is across the Pacific Ocean from Flores's homeland of the Philippines. It takes almost 20 hours to fly from one location to the other!

Today, the University of California has ten campuses across California. Flores attended the university's Berkeley location.

guests check in and out of the hotel. He carried their bags to and from their rooms. It was at this hotel that Flores would make toy history.

SOMETHING OLD,
Something New

One day in 1927, while taking a break at the hotel, Flores carved a wooden toy. It was made of simple round disks attached to a string. Flores held the string and dropped the disks, which spun and returned to his hand.

This toy was nothing new. In fact, it was a very popular toy known as a yo-yo back in the Philippines. But something about the toy he carved sparked the fascination of onlookers at the hotel.

Flores noticed that people were interested in his toy. He had recently read about a millionaire who got rich selling a hand game called paddleball. This game involved bouncing a ball attached to a

Philippine yo-yos were most often carved from wood or animal horn.

Flores printed pamphlets in 1928 describing scientific principles behind his toy and proper ways to use it.

rubber band off a paddle. Flores didn't expect to make millions of dollars. But he was tired of working for other people. He wanted to run his own business, and he knew his yo-yo had **potential**.

The Yo-Yo Manufacturing Company was born on June 9, 1928. Flores carved the company's first 12 yo-yos by hand. He then sold them to children in his neighborhood of Santa Barbara, California. The yo-yos were a huge hit! By November, Flores had already sold 2,000 of his toys.

ANCIENT
Success

It was no surprise that Flores's yo-yo became so popular. It is one of the oldest toys in the world! The first recorded yo-yos were used as early as 500 BCE.

Ancient Grecian **urns** show people playing with disks made of clay, wood, or metal. These disks were often painted with colorful images. A string was attached to their center.

By the 1500s, this disk toy had reached the Philippines. There it was named yo-yo, meaning "come-come" in the native language. Filipino children carved

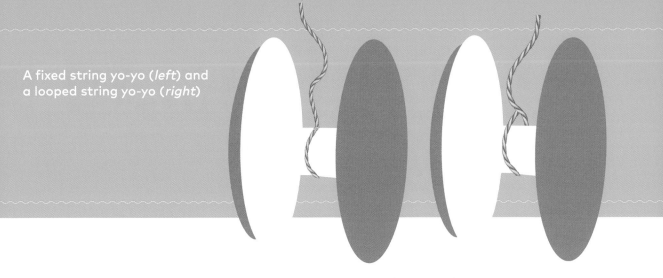

A fixed string yo-yo (*left*) and a looped string yo-yo (*right*)

their own yo-yos out of wood and bamboo. But they made a major improvement to the toy. Instead of fixing the string to the disk's center, they looped the string around it. This let the disk spin at the end of the string.

The yo-yo continued its journey to France in the 1700s, and then Great Britain. It was a popular toy among British royalty. In the 1860s, the yo-yo entered the United States.

Inventors James Haven and Charles Hettrick received the toy's first US patent in 1866. Other US inventors tried to improve the yo-yo's design. But the toy never became very popular. It would take Pedro Flores to kick-start the US yo-yo **craze**.

FUN FACT

The French gave the yo-yo many names. They called it the *bandalore*, *incroyable*, *emigrette*, and *joujou*.

Chapter 5

MACHINE-MADE *Marvels*

By November 1928, Flores had done what Haven and Hettrick couldn't do. He proved that the yo-yo could be popular in the United States. Investors took notice and helped finance the Yo-Yo Manufacturing Company. Flores used the money to buy machinery. His yo-yos were no longer hand carved. They were factory made!

By March, the company had sold 100,000 yo-yos. But Flores wanted to offer his customers a wider selection. Around this time, he hired designer Dorothy Carter. Carter designed yo-yos that appealed to many different customers. The simplest were sold for just 15 cents.

Flores carved his original yo-yos with a hand tool called a lathe. Each was made from one piece of wood and had a thin gap between disks.

Others were fancier, with silk strings. These cost as much as $1.50.

The yo-yo continued to rise in popularity. Over the next year, Flores expanded the company. He opened two new California factories. One was in Hollywood and the other was in Los Angeles. Between all three factories, Flores employed 600 people. Together, these workers produced 300,000 yo-yos each day.

Yo-Yo CONTEST CRAZE

Flores now had powerful machinery and many hardworking employees. Producing many yo-yos was easier than ever! But there was still plenty of work to do.

The yo-yo was a simple toy. What really amazed people was seeing it in action. Dropping a yo-yo so it spins back up was called throwing a yo-yo. Flores and his team knew that **demonstrating** yo-yos in public would boost

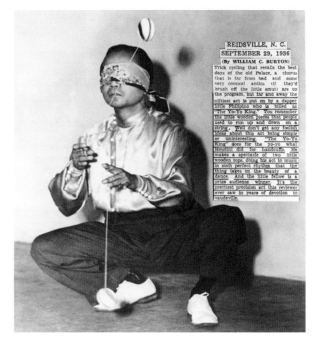

REIDSVILLE, N. C.
SEPTEMBER 29, 1936
(By WILLIAM C. BURTON)

Trick cycling that recalls the best days of the old Palace, a chorus that is far from bad and some very comical antics (if they'd brush off the little smut) are on the program, but far and away the niftiest act is put on by a dapper little Philipino who is billed as "The Yo-Yo King." You remember the little wooden pieces that people used to run up and down on a string. Well don't get any foolish ideas about this act being simple or uninteresting. "The Yo-Yo King" does for the yo-yo what Houdini did for handcuffs. He makes a spectacle of two little wooden tops, doing his act to music in such perfect rhythm that the thing takes on the beauty of a dance. And the little fellow is a prize audience winner. It's the prettiest precision act this reviewer ever saw in years of devotion to vaudeville.

Yo-yo contests continued into the 1930s. A newspaper clipping depicts a Filipino thrower performing during a 1936 contest.

Yo-yo contests were open to contestants of all ages.

sales. And they knew just the place to do it.

Flores teamed with movie theaters to hold yo-yo contests. At these contests, company employees showed attendees how to use yo-yos. Then they sold yo-yos to interested viewers. They could sell hundreds of yo-yos at these events!

At first, the yo-yo contests focused on endurance. Contestants competed to throw for the longest time. Eventually, the contests focused more on **technique**. Winners performed the most tricks without errors. Soon, other groups began holding yo-yo contests. By the end of 1929, newspapers across the country were calling the yo-yo the latest big fad.

Chapter 7

The DUNCAN Era

Flores's company became known for its quality toys. Flores knew his success would attract competitors. He wanted buyers to know, "If it isn't Flores, it isn't a yo-yo." This was his **slogan**. So, on July 22, 1930, Flores **trademarked** his toy. Now, no one else could sell yo-yos under his name.

Soon after, Flores teamed up with **entrepreneur** Donald F. Duncan. Duncan was an

Duncan Toys adapted Flores's slogan to include the company's name. The slogan became, "If it isn't a Duncan, it isn't a yo-yo."

experienced businessman. He was very impressed with Flores's toy. He wanted to make the yo-yo even more successful.

Meanwhile, Flores's passion had shifted. He was more interested in teaching children how to use yo-yos than in selling them. Flores's home life also changed around this time. In 1931, he married Edria Myers. The two were together the rest of Flores's life.

In 1929, Duncan bought Flores's company. It became the Duncan Toys Company. Flores continued to promote the company's yo-yos. One of his greatest successes was the Duncan Toys yo-yo team.

Flores gathered a group of yo-yo throwers that included his childhood friend Joseph Radovan. These throwers were Filipino **immigrants**, just like Flores. They had grown up playing with yo-yos. These throwers traveled the globe promoting Duncan Toys. They performed yo-yo tricks outside of stores selling yo-yos. Passersby were amazed at their skills. The throwers then encouraged viewers to buy yo-yos of their own.

Chapter 8

Read
ALL ABOUT IT

Duncan wasted no time leading the company forward. Right away, he acquired the rights to the word "yo-yo." Competitors now had to come up with new names for their toys. Duncan also released a new type of yo-yo, the O-Boy Yo-Yo Top. The O-Boy was similar to the Flores Yo-Yo. It was very popular. In 1931, the company sold 3 million in a single month!

Yo-yo sales continued to do well, even when the US **economy** entered a period of struggle. The **Great Depression** was a time in the 1930s when several nations' economies were poor. Few people had money to spare. But yo-yos were affordable for many people. The toy's popularity grew.

Much of the yo-yo's success was due to Duncan's **marketing** skills. Duncan Toys teamed

FUN FACT

Duncan paid Flores $250,000 for the Yo-Yo Manufacturing Company.

The yo-yo's popularity also rose in other countries during the Great Depression. A 1932 ad encourages buyers in London, England, to take part in the toy trend.

up with the Hearst newspaper chain. Hearst promoted Duncan's famous yo-yo contests in its papers. In return, contest entrants had to sell three newspaper **subscriptions** in order to compete. Hearst papers also ran Duncan Toys ads. The ads featured eye-catching images and catchy phrases.

Chapter 9

Supply Struggles

By the 1930s, much of Flores's work for Duncan was behind the scenes. He was no longer in the yo-yo spotlight. However, his success had inspired Radovan to start his own yo-yo company. In 1935, Radovan opened Royal Tops Manufacturing Company. Meanwhile, Flores continued to promote exciting events for Duncan Toys.

But the yo-yo business was not all fun and games. In 1939, **World War II** began. The US military needed all the supplies it could get. So the government **rationed** certain goods. It was difficult for yo-yo companies to get the materials that they needed to make toys.

Rationing ended soon after the war did in 1945. Duncan Toys returned to its normal operations. But it now had more competition. Radovan's yo-yos had risen in popularity. Flores wanted to help his friend. He began working with Radovan. As the **economy** improved, even more yo-yo companies popped up.

FUN FACT

In 1946, Duncan moved his factory to Luck, Wisconsin. This area had many maple trees. Their wood was used to create Duncan yo-yos. In Luck, Duncan Toys produced 3,600 yo-yos per hour! Today, the city is known as the yo-yo capital of the world.

Plastic allowed yo-yo makers to add new colors and improve performance.

Yo-yo buyers now had several choices. Duncan had to keep releasing new, exciting toys to compete for buyers. So, in the 1950s, he made a major change. Instead of wood, Duncan Toys began using plastic. Plastic yo-yos were lighter and easier to use. The new yo-yos were very popular.

Chapter 10

HOW IT'S MADE

Plastic yo-yos are made using many machines. Workers put several pieces together in an assembly line. The final product is shipped to toy stores around the world.

PLASTIC DISKS:

1. Plastic **pellets** are melted in a heated funnel.

2. A long, rotating screw pushes the melted plastic into a mold.

3. Tubes surrounding the mold fill with cold water. This cools the plastic.

4. The mold opens. Two outer shells and two flat disks fall onto an assembly line.

AXLES:

1. A long metal rod is cut into even sections. Each section will be an axle.

2. Each axle is fed into a clamp. Notches are cut into each end. These help the axle grip the plastic. The axles fall onto an assembly line.

ASSEMBLY:

1. A worker attaches each shell to its disk.

2. Next, a worker hammers the axle into one of the halves. He or she then hammers the remaining half onto the other end of the axle.

3. The yo-yo is fed into a machine press. The press further secures the yo-yo halves to the axle.

4. A spool of string is cut and looped around the axle.

5. A worker uses a special machine to spin the string onto the yo-yo.

6. The yo-yo is packaged and boxed for shipping!

Chapter 11

UPS and DOWNS

After years in the background, Flores was ready to shine again. In 1954, he started a new yo-yo company. He called it the Flores Corporation of America. But the Flores Corporation could not compete with Duncan Toys. Its products were largely ignored. The Flores Corporation's failure marked the end of Flores's amazing career. He lived his later years in Coshocton, Ohio. Flores died in December 1963.

In 1957, Duncan passed his toy company to his sons, Donald Jr. and Jack. At first, the company did very well. It released a new yo-yo, the Butterfly, that became very popular. Between 1962 and 1963, Duncan Toys sold 101 million Butterfly yo-yos!

But the company's success did not last. Production and **marketing** costs were too high. And Duncan Toys had spent too much money protecting its rights to the word yo-yo in previous years. In 1965, the company went **bankrupt**. Three years later, Flambeau Plastics Corporation bought the Duncan brand.

Flambeau could provide the plastics needed to create yo-yos. And now it had all the Duncan Toys molds and materials to continue the

The shape of a Duncan Butterfly yo-yo (*right*) is a traditional yo-yo (*left*) with the halves facing the opposite direction.

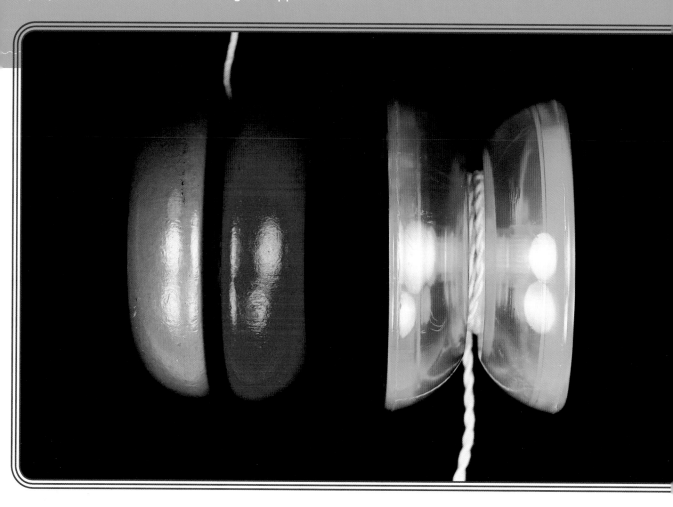

Duncan tradition. In 1999, the Duncan Yo-Yo entered the National Toy Hall of Fame. Duncan yo-yos are still made and sold today!

Chapter 12

The Modern THROWER

Pedro Flores fulfilled his dream of starting a business. In the process, he spread lasting joy around the nation. Today, a huge community of throwers meets at contests and **conventions** to celebrate their favorite toy. And for some, throwing is more than a game. It is a lifestyle.

Some professional throwers devote their lives to the art of throwing. In many ways, they take after Flores's original all-star team. Modern yo-yo pros participate in competitions around the world. Many of the contests are **sponsored** by yo-yo companies. Throwers at these contests try out new yo-yo models and represent certain companies.

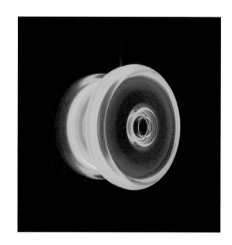

Many of today's yo-yos have supercool features, such as disks that light up as they spin.

Throwers have names for the tricks they perform. These include "sleeper," "brain twister," and "boingy boing"!

Today's yo-yos have come a long way from simple wooden disks. They are made for speed and **durability**. Most consist of metal or heavy plastic. The heavier weight helps them spin longer than wooden yo-yos. These pro yo-yos are more like tools than toys. Some cost hundreds of dollars!

From beginners to pro throwers, there is a yo-yo for everyone. And that was always Flores's goal. His enthusiasm and **marketing** skills sparked an unstoppable hobby. It is clear that the yo-yo is here to stay!

TIMELINE

1899

Pedro Flores is born in Vintar, Ilocos Norte, Philippines.

1915

Flores moves to the United States.

1929

Donald Duncan buys the Yo-Yo Manufacturing Company. He changes its name to the Duncan Toys Company.

500 BCE

The yo-yo is invented in ancient Greece.

1928

Flores starts the Yo-Yo Manufacturing Company on June 9.

1950s

Duncan Toys begins making plastic yo-yos.

1963

Flores dies in December.

1954

Flores starts the Flores Corporation of America.

1968

Flambeau Plastics Corporation buys Duncan Toys.

1999

The Duncan Yo-Yo enters the National Toy Hall of Fame.

Glossary

annex – to take land and add it to a nation.

bankrupt – legally declared unable to pay something owed.

convention – a group of people meeting for a special purpose.

craze – something that is very popular, often for a short time.

demonstrate – to show or explain, especially by using examples.

durability – the ability to exist for a long time without weakening.

economy – the way a nation produces and uses goods, services, and natural resources.

entrepreneur – one who organizes, manages, and accepts the risks of a business or an enterprise.

Great Depression – the period from 1929 to 1942 of worldwide economic trouble. There was little buying or selling, and many people could not find work.

immigrant – a person who enters another country to live.

marketing – the activities done to make buyers aware of and want to buy a service or product.

pellet – a small, hard ball.

Philippine-American War – a war between the First Philippine Republic and the United States, fought from February 1899 to July 1902.

potential – the capability or possibility of being or becoming.

province – a political division of a country.

ration – to control the amount of something people are allowed to have.

slogan – a word or a phrase used to express a position, a stand, or a goal.

Spanish-American War – a war between the United States and Spain in 1898. At the end of the war, Spain freed Cuba. It also signed over Guam, the Philippines, and Puerto Rico to the United States.

sponsor – to pay for a program or an activity in return for promoting a product or a brand.

subscription – the right to receive a publication, obtained by paying in advance. Subscriptions are often for a set number of newspaper or magazine issues.

technique (tehk-NEEK) – a method or style in which something is done.

trademark – something such as a word that identifies a certain company. It cannot be used by others without permission.

urn – a container that is often shaped like a vase and has a closed top. Urns are often used to hold the ashes of someone who has been cremated.

World War II – from 1939 to 1945, fought in Europe, Asia, and Africa. Great Britain, France, the United States, the Soviet Union, and their allies were on one side. Germany, Italy, Japan, and their allies were on the other side.